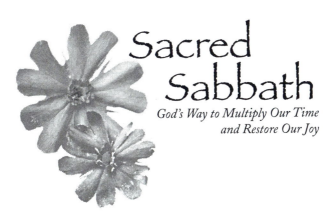

Sacred Sabbath

*God's Way to Multiply Our Time
and Restore Our Joy*

THE TEN COMMANDMENTS SERIES

MARJA MEIJERS

Tate Publishing, LLC

DEDICATION

My husband and I would like to dedicate this book to
the Swift family, who always supported us and made
our residency in California possible.

Maya Meyers

TABLE OF CONTENTS

Foreword 7

Introduction 11

Statement 17

PART I

1. The Lord says..23
2. If you treat the Sabbath as sacred 31
3. Do not pursue your own interests on that day ...39
4. If you value My Holy Day and honor it 47
5. Not traveling, working
   or talking idly on that day.................................55

PART II

6. Then you will find the joy 67
7. That comes from serving Me............................77
8. I will make you honored all over the world 87
9. You will enjoy the land I gave to your ancestor, Jacob. 95
10. I, the Lord, have spoken.................................107

FOREWORD

When I first read Marja's book "Sacred Sabbath," I literally had no idea how profound the impact of this manuscript would be. Even though I have pastored a church and been in ministry for over 20 years, I found myself receiving new insights and principles to approach the Sabbath. Her style of writing and accuracy of Scripture immediately started to quench a thirst inside of me as I read each page. It was so enlightening that I read the book in one sitting.

I believe this book is loaded with life changing nuggets. Marja's low-key, down-to-earth style helps the reader become very comfortable, as if you were sitting down having a cup of coffee or tea with her. I believe she is a fresh voice and a much-needed one. Over the years, I have seen Marja grow into a woman of impeccable faith. I have had the privilege of having lunch with her and her husband, Jan, and they both made a great impact on my life. What she writes in this book, she lives. I believe her being relaxed, easy-going, never in a hurry, always having time for friends and family, and yet found time to write this powerful book is a testimony to how special she is.

My wife, Kimberly, and I have always felt she was destined to do big things. This book is just one of the many big and impactful things she will accomplish with her life. If you are serious about change, this book will help mentor you in a way that you have never dreamed of. I believe it is one that will help you reach a fulfilled life.

If you read it, your eyes will be opened to a new level of living, a new level of peace that comes only when you see the Sabbath as sacred.

Pastor Lonnie G. McCowan D.D.,J.D.
Solid Rock Christian Center, Ventura, CA, Pastor

The Lord says, "If you treat the Sabbath as sacred and do not pursue your own interests on that day; if you value My Holy Day and honor it by not traveling, working or talking idly on that day, then you will find the joy that comes from serving Me. I will make you honored all over the world and you will enjoy the land I gave to your ancestor, Jacob. I, the Lord, have spoken."

Isaiah 58:13–14

INTRODUCTION

This book is a message given by the Holy Spirit, and I pray that its inspiration will catch on!

God planned this book perfectly. He gave me the idea to write a message about Isaiah 58:13–14. One morning my husband and I were sitting at the breakfast table studying the Bible and praying, when somehow we came across this Scripture. I heard an unmistakable voice inside my spirit. "This is your book." Like many other people, I have had the desire to write a book since I was a child. I just love the written word. I published my own magazine when I was about eight years old! The love for the written word was expressed in my involvement in school publications, church flyers, business news letters, etc. Writing travel diaries, short stories, and even a poem here and there was more than a hobby; it turned out to be my passion. Somehow, a real fresh idea, something worth publishing for a greater public, never came up. Looking back, it is easy to see how God gave me the ability to write (first of all in my own language, Dutch) and many opportunities to practice.

In the church where my husband and I attend while residing in California, the Solid Rock Christian Center in Ventura, we recently received a teaching about open doors and opportunities. Being in the internship program in this church, Pastor Lonnie McCowan promised us at the beginning of the 2004 semester the necessary support in case any of us wanted to write and publish a book. Right there and then, it came to my mind; this is my chance! Still, I had a hundred excuses not to start right away. What subject? Will people read it? I don't have a computer, etc. That one morning at the breakfast table the door opened for the real thing, the real work! I wrote down that Scripture on a piece of paper, and we immediately prayed over it. We thanked God for the idea, we prayed for wisdom and inspiration, we blessed the work of my hands, and we declared it a bestseller, right there and then, before one word was written down. The book was there in the spiritual; it was my job to give it form in the natural!

When God wants His work to be done, He has it all figured out long before we realize what is happening. He is the best logistics manager I have ever known! The idea was provided, the inspiration, the support, even the tools were provided. A dear brother and sister from the Agape church in Holland came for a visit to California, and they blessed us with a brand new laptop computer to work with. It seemed everything was prepared, but the labor itself. When things line up as described above, there are no more excuses: there is work to do! When God has a message for His people, He uses someone to proclaim it, just as in Old Testament times. He uses a messenger, a prophet, many times one that has no clue as of what to say or how to explain things. In this case, someone who does not even master the language perfectly, someone who has never written a book before and who never spoke to an entire generation.

I simply wrote down what He wanted me to write

down. The subject has never before been on my mind. Believe me when I say it would be the last thing I wanted to write about. We had no real opinion about the Sabbath, until my husband and I came to the USA and noticed that there was not even room for a Sabbath in her 24/7 society. The term "a day of rest" had disappeared, even within Christian circles. We simply regarded that phenomenon as a cultural difference, until the day the Lord gave us His message. It is not deep, it is not very spiritual, and it is no mind-boggling revelation. It is His message, and I see it as my assignment to give it to you and to make you think about it. His message still has the power to change lives and ultimately that of a nation!

Marja Meijers

Sab·bath (sab th), *n*. [ME. *sabat* < OFr. & AS. *sabat;* both < L. *sabbatum;* Gr. *sabbaton;* Heb. *shabb th* < *sh bath*, to rest], 1. the seventh day of the Jewish week, set aside by the fourth Commandment for rest and worship; Saturday. 2. Sunday: name applied by most Protestant denominations. 3. [s-], a period of rest. *Adj.* of the Sabbath. Abbreviated **S., Sab.**

STATEMENT

৯†৵

Before you start reading this book, it is important to take notice of the following statement. As the title of this book suggests, this is a book about the Sabbath and keeping it holy. This is NOT a book about rules! The Bible says in Colossians 2:16–17,

So let no one make rules about what you eat or drink or about holy days or the New Moon Festival or the Sabbath. All such things are only a shadow of things in the future; the reality is Christ.

Whether it is your custom to regard the Saturday or Sunday as Sabbath is of no importance to the message that I want to bring across. The main point to be made is the fact that the seventh day of the week has been set apart by God Himself as holy, as a day of rest and that we can choose to treat it as such in order to receive the blessings as promised by God. If it is your custom to go to church on a Sunday, then that is the sacred day. If it is your custom to go to church on Saturday, then that is the sacred day. I certainly do not want to talk "Sabbathology."

It is not my intention to discuss the differences between Old and New Testament and whether God speaks to Jews, Christians, or nonbelievers. I do not want to discuss whether modern day Christians are required to keep the whole law, parts of the law, or nothing at all because they are set free. These are interesting questions and worth debating, but not in this book. This book is a simple but clear message from God, in the first place to Christians in America and all over the world. It is a personal message for whoever wants to hear it out. I want to be personal to whoever thinks this is worthwhile listening to. I am speaking to YOU, and only you must decide to take this message or leave it.

If you are curious and ready to receive an uncommon thought, I urge you to pray this prayer before you start reading; it will help you.

Dear Father in Heaven, I honor You and I honor Your Word. I thank you for Your everlasting LOVE for me. Holy Spirit, help me to open up my mind for this message. I want to fulfill God's Word by living it! I pray this in Jesus name. Amen.

4ᵗʰ COMMANDMENT

"Observe the Sabbath and keep it holy. You have six days in which to do your work, but the seventh day is a day of rest dedicated to Me. On that day no one is to work – neither you, your children, your slaves, your animals, nor the foreigners who live in your country. In six days I, the Lord, made the earth, the sky, the seas, and everything in them, but on the seventh day I rested. That is why I, the Lord, blessed the Sabbath and made it holy."

Exodus 20:8–11

PART 1

The Lord says, "If you treat the Sabbath as sacred and do not pursue your own interests on that day; if you value My Holy Day and honor it by not traveling, working or talking idly on that day . . ."

Isaiah 58:13

1

The Lord says

Listen, then, if you have ears!

Matthew 13:9

The passage in Isaiah 58:13 is a direct message from God to the reader, you! It opens up with the words: *The Lord says . . .* Maybe it is not the common way to start a book by asking you to stop and think a while about the first sentence, but then, this book is not about the common way.

It is of great importance to sit down, take your time, and think for a while about the true meaning behind a little sentence like this. "The Lord says" implies the spoken word. God speaks a word. It is up to us whether we want to listen or not. When God speaks, He creates. He brings something into existence just as He created light by using words. We can find praise for His creating power in Psalm 148. The writer urges all creation to glorify God. In verse 5, he explains the reason for this worship.

Let them all praise the name of the Lord! He commanded, and they were created.

God created more than the heavens and the earth. He spoke laws, promises, and truths into existence.

These are written down in His Word for the reader to meditate on and live by.

Notice that Isaiah 58:13–14 is written in present tense and that He addresses YOU. Please, do not read this with the word "history" all over it. Read it as if someone is giving you the message today. God speaks throughout the entire Old Testament in various ways. He speaks through the leaders of Israel, through prophets, angels, and believe it or not, even through a donkey (see the story in Numbers 22). In the New Testament, God still speaks. He speaks through His Son, Jesus, and later on through the apostles. In Matthew 24:35 the importance and power of God's words are made clear in a strong statement of Jesus.

Heaven and earth will pass away, but My words will never pass away.

On many occasions, Jesus told His disciples about the importance of His words, which were the words of God Himself. In John 7:16, He says,

"What I teach is not My own teaching, but it comes from God, who sent Me."

In this 21st century God still speaks to us through His written Word, the Bible.
Whether you read the Bible regularly, hardly ever open it up, or never read a word into it does not change the message of the Bible. You might not read it, but millions of people all over the world do. More and more people start reading the Bible in an ongoing quest for answers to their problems and questions.

This could be a good moment to pick up a translation that speaks to your age and lifestyle, and give it a try. In this book, I purposely used, unless otherwise noted, the Today's English Version (also known as the Good News version), because it really opened my eyes with its simple, down-to-earth, yet powerful style. Since English is not my native tongue, I need clear and simple words. Picking up the Good News changed everything I ever heard or read before.

I want to ask you a simple question: Do you believe that the Bible is God's Word and do you want to take His Word seriously? Be honest when you think this over. We might have a tendency to only take seriously what appeals to us or what we think is useful or easily applicable in life. We reason that to be able to take every word seriously we need divine thinking and God's wisdom flowing through us at all times. In other words, we like to use our humanity as an excuse to take from His Word what we like and what is understandable and to ignore the passages we do not like or that do not seem to fit in our modern-day society. We like to regard these passages as mere history or theology.

We have to look into God's Word to find answers that can change our way of thinking. In 1 Corinthians 2:16b, a powerful statement is made by the Apostle Paul.

We, however, have the mind of Christ.

What made Paul say that? Can Christians, as followers of Jesus, truly have the mind of Christ? John

25

15:15 (NIV) explains this clearly through the words of Jesus when He promises His followers:

I no longer call you servants, because a servant does not know his master's business. Instead, I have called you friends, for everything that I learned from My Father I have made known to you.

Through Jesus everything was made known to us. Awesome statement, isn't it? Everything was made known to us, that is, if we accept His friendship. He calls us His friends. He never said we couldn't be. His offer still stands today. He never changes His mind; we do! His invitation is simple; all we have to do is decide if we want to be His friend too! Maybe you never thought about becoming friends with Jesus. Well, it doesn't matter that His words were spoken 2000 years ago; they are still valid. If you want to be a part of Jesus' circle of friends, all you have to do is say aloud (anytime) that Jesus is Lord, and you have to believe (all the time) that God raised Him from the dead.

You may think this is so simple; it is almost ridiculous. There must be more to it. What about forgiveness of my sins and all that? Listen, you ARE forgiven! Yes, the Bible tells us to stop our wicked ways, to turn our life into another direction. Saying aloud that Jesus is Lord is not just a simple statement. It means that sin is no longer lord in our lives. It means that we will obey Him and no longer our own desires. It means a shift in our lives, a shift in the direction we are going. A shift that we will never regret! If you are honest about your confession, it will work for you. Underline

Romans 10:9–10 in your Bible if you haven't done so already.

If you confess that Jesus is Lord and believe that God raised Him from death, you will be saved. For it is by our faith that we are put right with God; it is by our confession that we are saved.

Saying aloud (and meaning it) that Jesus is Lord will change your life forever. Aren't you glad you don't have to jump through hoops, prepare a speech, or get a goofy haircut (not to talk about paying a membership fee) to be part of Jesus' friends? Through Jesus, everything was made known to us! So if there are things we do not understand or grasp yet, don't worry! The longer we hang out with Him, the longer we are His friends, then the more we will see things become clear. Do not worry about lack of knowledge or lack of understanding. The Bible will turn out to be a never-ending source of information, wisdom, and personal teaching. God is not a mysterious God somewhere, far away on His own safe planet. He made Himself known to us through the Old Testament. Then He sent His Son Jesus to earth to be our example. He was crucified for our sins and sicknesses and was raised up from the dead after three days to sit again at the right side of God. After that, God has sent the Holy Spirit to live inside believers so they can still communicate with the Father and the Son. In John 14:26 Jesus says,

The Helper, the Holy Spirit, whom the Father will send in My name, will teach you everything and make you remember all that I have told you.

Never be discouraged!
I wrote all this to put emphasis on the words written in Hebrews 4:12 (NIV):

For the Word of God is living and active. Sharper than any double-edged sword,

He wants us to read it, live it, and spread it. It is as applicable today as it was over 2000 years ago. It speaks to individuals in a present tense. It speaks to whoever is willing to hear and understand at any given moment.

It really helps me to fill in my own name wherever possible, when reading the Bible, to make it more personal. When reading the Word aloud and filling in your own name, you can hear God speaking to you anytime. No longer do you need to say, "I cannot hear God. I do not understand Him. I never hear His voice." His voice is written down for all generations! All you have to do is read it aloud and personalize it. God speaks to you in ways you can never imagine. His Word truly comes to life at your dining room table, at your computer desk, in your bedroom, in the living room, up in the mountains, on the beach, or wherever you study. Remember that whenever you want or need to hear from Him, simply open up His living Word, read aloud, and listen!
The Lord says . . .

Meditate on the following:

❖ *Am I willing to believe that the whole Bible is God's Word?*

❖ *Do I truly realize that God can speak to me personally through His written Word? Do I dare to fill in my own name?*

❖ *How do I value the Bible from a historical, literal, and moral perspective?*

Journal your thoughts:

2

If you treat the Sabbath as sacred

*I find pleasure in obeying Your commands, because I love
them. I respect and love Your commandments; I will
meditate on Your instructions.*

Psalm 119:47–48

If you love Me, you will obey My commandments.

John 14:15

God speaks to us when we read Isaiah 58:13–14. He
speaks to us personally, but He also speaks to a nation
that reads His Word. Today He speaks to a generation that is struggling with stress, too little time to
get everything done, and the ever-present feeling
that life is slipping through her hands.

I believe God gave us guidelines to prevent this frus-
trating kind of living. In Isaiah 58:13–14, He makes
us an offer we cannot refuse. He wants us to have a
day of rest every 7th day, dedicated to Him. He promises us joy and honor in return. You may ask how He
knew where we would end up in the 21st century?
Did He already know that we would be running out
of time? Did He truly foresee that stress would be
an almost incurable disease in our modern-day society? If He foresaw that, why didn't He do something
about it right then? Why does He let us suffer and

31

make a mess of our lives? Isn't He able to stop our self-destruction? He made us; shouldn't He be able to fix us too? Do you know where we will end up with questions like this? We will end up in the Bible. God did indeed foresee our troubles. That is why He gave us guidelines. That is why He counseled us before we even asked for help. That is why He has given us a manual when He assembled our lives.

He has given us inside knowledge on how to avoid stress (and many more things besides that). Our problem is that we find it so hard to understand the language, as in the manual that comes with a new television set or washing machine. We get irritated before we even start reading! That is how we often handle God's Word. We hardly ever give Him the chance to speak up. We interrupt Him after hearing the first sentence. "Oh, God, don't give me that. Don't burden me with religious nonsense. I really don't need to be told what to do and what not to do. I am a grown up." Yes, we are afraid He wants to burden us with rules and regulations. That is the last thing we need; we want to be free!

Haven't we all been there at some time in our lives? We are proud of our independent lives and our self-supportiveness. Yes, we are even proud of all the self-help books we have read and the pages with truly useful advice we have found while surfing the web. We know our way around this world. We know all about time management and multitasking. We have become masters in planning and scheduling. Who doesn't have a full calendar page each week on the refrigerator door or a digital agenda in the laptop or a weekly schedule at the office? Wherever we go, our hours seem to be planned by others: opening and closing hours in the stores, office hours at the bank and the post office, class schedules at the gym, appointment openings at the doctor's office, etc. Our days are filled from morning to evening. We have arrived, haven't we?

I know I speak for many when I make the statement that somehow the big question still remains: If we're all so busy moving, what are we headed toward? Where are we going? Are we able to define our destination? Why the rush? When are we supposed to be there? If we are so capable of running our own lives, how come we end up tired, stressed out, overwhelmed, and sometimes even depressed? How come we hardly ever get the feeling that we are where we want to be? Where did we go wrong?

Oh, if we would only take some time to listen. Someone wants to talk to us. Someone has wanted to talk to us for a long, long time. God knows our busy lives, our hectic schedules and our longing for some rest and peace. He knew. He knew all along. That is why He wants to talk to us about time, about the days that make up a week, about the weeks that make up our lives.

You may think the God of the Old Testament doesn't have the answers for your problems today. After all, it was a different time, and it seems that people spend their precious time fighting violent wars, setting up camp, watering their gardens, and maybe counting cattle. No sight yet of a 24/7 society: weekend jobs, endless social obligations, frequent credit problems that take up time and effort, and on top of that, sport games and new movies to watch every week! Will the God of Abraham, Isaac, and Jacob be able to help us today to live a happy, relaxed, and peaceful life? The answer is yes. He is as serious about guiding us today as He was about guiding His beloved people thousands of years ago. Do we want to hear what He has to say? Are we open to suggestions?

When reading the first part of the Scripture in Isaiah 58:13, God starts talking to us immediately and opens up with the word if. He is not commanding. He is not asking. He is not warning. The way I personally read it is as if He is trying to make a deal with me. If you do this and this . . . , He does not yell or bark His orders. He merely wants to give us a little secret or inside knowledge. He is trying to give us help to live our daily lives. I do know enough of God to realize that when He says "if," He is serious in teaching me a principle, a law, a lesson. If He starts like that, He has my full attention. I hope He has yours too!

He starts immediately with a proposal. Let's say we do not know what comes next; we do not know what the second part of the Scripture is. Let us just concentrate on this particular sentence in Isaiah 58:13.

If you treat the Sabbath as sacred

First of all, God speaks about the Sabbath here. We have to go to the fourth of the Ten Commandments to learn more about the Sabbath. Only the second and fourth commandments are considerably longer than the rest. More words were needed to describe the commandments about worshiping idols and keeping the Sabbath holy than were needed for the other eight. This fact shows me that God is serious about the Sabbath. In Exodus 20:8–10 God says,

Observe the Sabbath and keep it holy. You have six days in which to do your work, but the seventh day is a day of rest dedicated to Me.

He goes on from there with instructions and explanations regarding that special day. As I wrote earlier in this book, I leave it up to you which day is the Sabbath. The point of view that I have taken in this book is that after every six-day work week He established a day of rest. Not just an ordinary day of rest though, He wants us to dedicate that day to Him. You probably think, Oh my! Being a Christian is already a full-time job; it is a lifestyle. Does God want more? In Matthew 10:39 (NIV), Jesus says,

Whoever loses his life for My sake will find it.

Yes, He wants all of our time, our whole life. At the same time, He promises something in return. God wants us to have more! He wants to help us by giving specific guidelines for His special day!

So He wants us to recognize a Sabbath day, a day of rest after every six days. He wants us to treat that day as sacred. Sacred means to set apart. He wants that day to be different from the rest of our days. Unmistakably different! Don't worry yet as on how to fill that in; God gives us tips and advice. Just try to concentrate on the first part of this Scripture where God starts to set up His deal with us. I want to be sure that you meditate on this part of Isaiah 58:13, not just read it and forget it. I want you to forget about rules and regulations. While reading this book I want you to forget what you may already know about God's Holy Day. Maybe you should even forget the way you grew up with or without a holy day. I want you to think about what God is going to offer you. He wants to make an offer you cannot refuse. Are you ready for that?

To continue on to the next part of our foundation Scripture, we need to make up our mind concerning the two things God talks about when He says *"If you treat the Sabbath as sacred . . ."*

The first one: We need a Sabbath (a day of rest) every 7th day. After all, if Almighty God wanted rest after working six days, what makes us think we can do without? We are made in His image, aren't we? I am sure God didn't need the rest; He is God! However, I understand He wanted to set an example for generations to come. When God created the whole universe, He designed everything very carefully. We only need to look around us at mountains, deserts, oceans, a tiny butterfly, a giant lion, and at people with their unique characters. Not a single person on earth is the same as another one! There is only one of you! Think about the greatness of our universe, the galaxies, and the stars and planets; everything has been handled with care! God designed the hours of our days, the days of our weeks, and the months that make up a year. Part of that design was the seventh day, which He blessed and called a special day because by that day He had completed His creation and stopped working. You can find that in Genesis 2:3.

The second one: We need to treat that day as sacred. We need to set it apart by dedicating it to God.

Meditate on the following:

❖ *Am I ready to believe that I need a day of rest after every six-day period?*

❖ *Am I willing to dedicate that day to the Lord?*

❖ *What does it mean for me to dedicate a day to the Lord?*

Journal your thoughts:

3

Do not pursue your own interests on that day

We should not please ourselves. Instead, we should all please our brothers for their own good, in order to build them up in the faith. For Christ did not please Himself.

Romans 15:2

᧤✝᧥

This chapter is going to be a tough one. Most of us probably love to talk about our own interests, and it has been one of our goals in life to pursue them. After all, it is our lives, our futures, and we want to make the best of it.

Well, no reason for panic so far; pursuing our interests is in itself a good thing. God created each human being with interests, desires, talents, and skills in order to be able to fulfill His divine plan, His purpose for every one of us. Psalm 139:16 says,

You saw me before I was born. The days allotted to me had all been recorded in your book, before any of them ever began.

It would be disappointing to Him if we didn't go after that purpose, the plan He has for each one of us. He expects us, sooner or later, to discover the greater meaning of life!

In this part of Isaiah 58:13 God tells us not to pursue our own interests on that day, the sacred day, the Sabbath. This tells me I can pursue my own interests on other days. Doesn't it?

In order to understand God's way of thinking in this part of Scripture, we have to let go of our own. I am almost sure that you, like a lot of people, Christian or not, regard the Sabbath (or the Sunday) as a special day. It is after all part of the weekend and if you have the weekends off, you just want to do something fun on that day, like going fishing or watching a movie or going shopping—something you enjoy doing and something you don't have that much time for during the week, because you're working (either inside or outside the home) or going to school. Maybe you think Sundays are a blessing and a good excuse to get away from the house, the homework, or the family and do something for yourself. Now why would God tell us NOT to do something for ourselves? That doesn't make sense. You already made your Sunday a special day. Why change it? This reflects for most of us the common way of thinking. If for whatever reason we regard one day a week as special, we regard it as OUR special day, and thus we want to do the things we like or love. God's way of thinking, the uncommon way, goes like this: One day a week is special. It is not yours; it is MINE. Pursue Me and not your own interests.

I want you to think for a moment about the principle behind tithing (giving 10 percent of all your income to the Lord). God wants His children to tithe, to give 10 percent of all their blessings back to Him, so He can bless the other 90 percent! If we apply that to His Holy Day, the same principle will work. I am not focusing on percentages and numbers here, but on giving in order to receive. If we give Him back one day a week, He can bless the other six! Interesting thought, isn't it? If it works with our money, why wouldn't it work with our time?

Let us go back to our daily lives. Just talk to anybody in the street, the store, or even the church. Doesn't it seem to you that everybody is busy? Doesn't it seem to you that everybody needs more time? Could it be that we lack time during the week because we are trying to keep ALL the days for ourselves, because we refuse to give God His rightful one day a week? If God gives us the advice not to pursue our own interests on that day but dedicate it to Him, wouldn't He have something special in mind? Wouldn't He be able to bless the other six days in which we do pursue our own interests? I think we are robbing God from His special day as we would be robbing God if we don't pay back the 10 percent of our increase to Him. In Malachi 3:9, God says we are under a curse because we are robbing Him.

Throughout this book and hopefully throughout the rest of your life, I want to challenge you. If you are one out of those millions of people who are often busy and hardly ever have enough time to get everything done, start giving back to God His special day. Just try it for a season. You will find out He starts to bless the other six days in a supernatural way. You will always have enough time!

In Chapter 2, I wrote about the two things we need to make up our mind about. The first one: We need a day of rest every 7th day. The second thing: We need to treat that day as sacred. If you decided positive on these, you are ready to go to the next level of commitment. Basically, God is saying that if we do not have a special day, we have to start announcing one, and if we have done so, not to use it for ourselves.

As I said in my statement at the beginning of this book, it is not my intention to give a list of rules and laws to make life miserable. This book is not about do's and don'ts. It is about common sense when listening to God. It is about receiving the blessings as promised by God.

If you are a person who often complains about being so busy and lacking the time to get everything done, stop complaining! It is not going to help you; it is certainly not going to change anything. Why not try what the Bible suggests? God's suggestion is not a rule to make your life more complicated; it is a lovely promise to make it more enjoyable! In Luke 11:46, Jesus very clearly rebuked the Pharisees about the regulations they wanted the people to obey. He told them,

You put onto people's backs loads which are hard to carry, but you yourselves will not stretch out a finger to help them carry those loads.

God is not like that. He does not want to burden us; He wants to guide and help us.

I simply want you to look into your own life and find out what kind of interests you normally pursue during the six days of work or school and maybe as well during the 7th day. Do you pursue your own interests during most of the week? Could you change your attitude on the Sabbath? That is the basic question you have to ask yourself. What do I do during the week? Am I willing NOT to do those things during the Sabbath? Again, this is not about good or bad, right or wrong. This is about common sense, God's common sense. Jesus asked the people if they were allowed to do good on the Sabbath, to help or harm (Mark 3:4). To "do" means action. You are not asked to be passive on that day. Resting does not mean to be lazy or to sleep. Resting means: to rest from your daily routines and work. Doing good means you can go and visit a friend who is sick or lonely. Doing good means you can go and help cook a meal for an elderly person or take someone who enjoys birds and flowers out for a hike in the hills. Doing good means to pursue someone else's interests, not your own. When God states that we should not pursue our own interests on that day, He gives us the opportunity to pursue HIS interests on that day!

His interest for example is in us loving Him, by going to His house for celebration, worship, paying tithes and offerings, and by receiving teaching. His interest is in us loving other people. God loves people and only by us showing care and love for one another does it show that we belong to Him. Romans 13:10 tells us,

If you love someone, you will never do him wrong; to

43

love, then, is to obey the whole Law.

Going to the mall and spending money on clothes and accessories is not on God's list of things to do for others. That is pursuing your own interest. Washing your car or painting your house is not on God's list of things to do for others. That is pursuing your own interest. Do you notice the common sense in this? There is nothing wrong with shopping or washing your car, but it is not what God has in mind for His special day. He wants us to focus on Him and others, which is basically the heart of Christianity and should be the focus of our lives all the time with God's special day, the Sabbath, as highlight, as celebration.

Giving 10 percent of your increase to God seems a minor gift if we think of the 90 percent we can keep and spend. After all, everything belongs to God as we can read in Romans 11:36,

For all things were created by Him, and all things exist through Him and for Him.

We are just using His resources and blessings. Giving Him one day and keeping the other six for our interests and work should not be too much to ask either. We would be out of our minds to complain about a deal like that. Give to God what belongs to Him! The Sabbath is His day; He calls it MY Holy Day. By giving Him the hours on that day, He will multiply them and give them back to you during the other days! You will never, ever run out of time again!

This may sound like a very bold statement to you, but

I am drawing from my own experience, and I am not afraid to proclaim God's way to be the truth. I am so excited about God's way to multiply our time that I have to contain myself not to scream this principle in people's faces when discussing their busy, busy lives. It works, believe it or not!

As a bonus, you will discover that when you give Him His Holy Day, it turns out to be much easier to live for Him the other six days of the week too. It becomes a lifestyle! You will discover that His way is the best way, the only satisfying way!

Meditate on the following:

❖ *How do I pursue my own interests?*

❖ *Could I use more time? If yes, for what reason?*

❖ *Can I think of something I can do for God on His special day?*

Journal your thoughts:

4

If you value My Holy Day and honor it

And My Father will honor anyone who serves Me.

John 12:26b

❧✝☙

Value is just how much you think something is worth. In this chapter, we need to ask ourselves, do I want to validate God's special day?

So far, I have asked you to meditate on announcing a Sabbath and on dedicating it to the Lord. I have asked you to think about pursuing your own interests versus pursuing God's interests. I hope and pray you have decided positively about this and announced a Sabbath in your life. If so, you are ready to go on to the next level of commitment to our part of this deal.

God wants us to value His Holy Day. What exactly is value, I had to ask myself. Do I have things of value? What do I value? Whom do I value? Not so long ago, I had to go to the store to get some new ink cartridges for my printer. While I was trying to find my way between the ridiculous amount of different brand names, shapes, colors, sizes, and prices, I noticed that buying a whole new printer was less expensive than buying two single cartridges. Best of all, the new printer came with two (!) new cartridges. I hesitated, not because I didn't think this was a good deal or I didn't want to buy a new printer, but because I was wondering about the value of an advanced high-tech machine like a printer versus a tiny black box with colors in it. Didn't we learn in school that "value" is the worth of a thing in money or goods at a certain time? I know that at a certain time, printers were expensive, especially the ones that were able to print a good color quality. Time changed and so the value changed. Not for the cartridges though, they were always expensive (as far back as I can remember).

The point I want to make is this: The word value did not change, but the things we regard as valuable have changed. In the 21st century we definitely do not put the same value tag on marriage that our grandparents did at the beginning of the previous century. We should not have changed the value, but it happened anyway. The same observation is applicable to family life. Maybe we wish we still had some of the so-called, old-fashioned family values, but we must face the truth—most of us don't. We somehow lost them along the way.

Think about sex. Once valued as precious communication in a marriage and a way to reproduce, nowadays it has been reduced by many to a way of getting what we want or a way of getting even with somebody who has hurt us. It is used as a way of trying to heal our own hurts and pains or as a way to feel accepted. Saddest of all, it is also used for marketing.

What used to be valuable has disappeared from our society or has been degraded to something about which we hardly ever think. We acknowledge the existence of certain things, but we forget to read the value tag. Therefore, we have no idea if we are willing to pay the price. Take marriage for an example again. We still acknowledge the institution of marriage; people get married every day. A lot of us, however, have no idea what the value tag is. We don't know if we are able to pay the price. We are greedy. We want to have it, we want the status that comes with it, and we want it NOW. Once we have obtained what we wanted (a certain person in our lives), we discover that we cannot afford it. We need to sacrifice to be able to pay the price.

God wants us to value His Holy Day. Just having that day is not enough, as being married is not enough for a good relationship. We have to value it! Just trying to keep the day for Him is not enough. He wants us to value it, to think highly of it. Reading through this book you might think, okay, it seems I need a special day dedicated to the Lord. Whatever. I'll set one up and get it over with. Maybe I will get something out of it after all. Listen—that is not the way God has it in mind. He wants us to value that day. Just keeping the Sabbath holy does not tell anything about our attitude. Just being married to someone doesn't tell anything about the way that relationship is going. A lot of Christians keep laws, regulations, and religious habits without knowing why. When asked, they simply reply, "My parents did it; everybody in my church does it." Or, "I don't know, I never thought about it really." So God doesn't just add this note as a less important remark. No, He puts emphasis on the point He wants to make. He does not want anybody just to do as He says with a "whatever" attitude. He very clearly specifies His desires and requests. He wants us to think about our actions and attitudes.

It may be helping you to think again about the principle of tithing. God doesn't just tell us to give; He prefers it a certain way. In 2 Corinthians 9:7 (KJV), we can read that . . .

God loves a cheerful giver.

He does not want us to give our tithes and offerings to Him out of duty or obligation or worse, because everybody does it. He wants us to give Him something because we love Him, because we appreciate Him, and because we are thankful to Him. He wants us to give happily! That is just the way He likes it.

I feel free to apply that same principle regarding the Sabbath. He wants us to value that day. He wants us to be serious about it. He doesn't want us to take it lightly. If you feel you would like to know more about the Sabbath, about the Jewish customs on that day, about historical value or theological views, please check out the Internet or the library. You probably need a lifetime to read everything that has ever been written about it. People have debated the Sabbath, argued about the value in our modern day, and questioned the true meaning. It is okay to study this subject further, to meditate on it, and to pray about it, as long as you keep the Bible as your reference guide. Being serious about God's Holy Day for starters is a way of valuing it.

In Webster's Dictionary, the verb "to value" is

explained as: to think highly of.[1] God wants us to think highly of His Holy Day. God further adds, " . . . and honor it." To honor something or someone can be done in many ways. In the next chapter, you will read how God has that in mind on this particular subject. For now, I want you to think about honor and its different meanings. According to Webster's, to honor is: [1]

1. to respect greatly; regard highly; esteem
2. to show great respect or high regard for; treat with deference and courtesy
3. to worship
4. to confer and honor on; exalt; ennoble
5. to accept and pay when due

Honor is a word and attitude that is slowly disappearing from our culture. Honoring parents, teachers, or leaders is not a popular subject. It seems to be replaced by indifference and selfishness. A popular slogan in modern-day society is: It is MY life and I do what I want. In other words, I am not going to listen to anybody. Mind your own business. I'll find out myself.
You will, indeed.

In Chapter 2, I described our society as one that is proud of her independence and self-help structure. We can figure it all out if given enough time and money! I think that a result of this same society is the fact that we find it very difficult to accept correction and guidance. After all, we want to find out ourselves. We do not like to be taken by the hand

[1] © 1960 Webster's New World Dictionary of the American Language college edition World Publishing Company, Cleveland & New York

and guided into a different direction. We do not want to go off our familiar track. What if we get lost? What if we meet strangers? We are self-supporting, and in case we really need somebody's help in certain troubled areas of our lives, we can always seek professional help. There seems to be therapy for about everything, but then again, we switch doctors and therapists as if they were a pair of jeans. If we don't like the direction they are sending us in, we leave. We keep looking for someone or something who will tell us what we want to hear! We go from yoga, to Pilates, to massage therapy, to psychics, even from church to church, searching for anything or anybody who will agree with the way we already think. Yes, we want our help to come from a direction that we choose. We want our help to come from a direction that we are comfortable with, something we can feel at peace with.

This attitude has already been foreseen in God's Word. In 2 Timothy 4:3, we can read the following warning:

The time will come when people will not listen to sound doctrine, but will follow their own desires and will collect for themselves more and more teachers who will tell them what they are itching to hear.

I think we should ask ourselves if we only honor the people and methods that somehow appeal to us. Are we able to honor somebody who corrects us, who guides us into an opposite direction?
Whether you grew up honoring the people around you or not, whether you know how to express honor

to somebody or not, please pay close attention as you move on to the next chapter. God is very specific on how to honor His way.

Meditate on the following:

❖ *What do I regard as valuable in my life?*

❖ *Do I do things in my life just because everybody does it?*

❖ *Do I honor God? If yes, how?*

Journal your thoughts:

5

Not traveling, working or talking idly on that day

Your instructions give me pleasure;
they are my advisers.

Psalm 119:24

ఞ†ఞ

We don't have to figure out how to honor God's special day! He has it all written down for us, very plain, very simple. It is up to us if we want to give it a try.

It has never been God's plan to make our lives miserable and complicated. He only wants the best for us. You probably heard that cliché many times before. Think for a moment about Genesis 1:27.

So God created human beings, making them to be like Himself.

It would be weird if God made us in His very own image, and at the same time expected us to live a miserable and difficult life. That does not make sense. We are made in His image to be like Him. In John 17:22, Jesus talks about the believers to His Father when He says,

I gave them the same glory You gave Me.

A more familiar Scripture can be found in John

10:10 where Jesus talks to us when He explains His purpose on earth.

I have come in order that you might have life–life in all its fullness.

If you have trouble believing that, there is always the other option as stated in the first part of that same Scripture.

The thief (devil) *comes only in order to steal, kill and destroy.*

Yes, there is someone out there to destroy our joy, our peace, and our lives.

I think it is very important, while thinking about honoring the Sabbath, that we keep John 10:10 in mind. It is NOT God's intention to make our lives miserable. He wants us to fully enjoy and live our lives. He is only trying to help us by setting up guide-lines. It is up to us to choose to follow them. Do we want to live by His guidance or don't we? Do we want the quality of our lives to be improved or don't we? In case of the Sabbath, do we want our time to be supernaturally blessed or don't we?

For centuries, people have been discussing God's Law, commandments, regulations, and guidelines. Somehow, God's orders were altered, changed, mis-understood, or simply ignored. Many people have been trying to be better people by telling others what to do and what not to do. Somehow, I think they have often been missing the point. God's guidelines are not about being a better person than the one next to you. God's guidelines are not about gaining favor with some folks around you or even with God Himself. He has set up His rules for the lives of His children, and in doing so, He gave them a way of expressing their love for Him. In 1 John 5:3 it says,

For our love for God means that we obey His commands. And His commands are not too hard for us.

Yes, we can express our love for God by obeying Him! His commands are about blessings; they are about a full life. In Isaiah 48:18, God says,

If only you had listened to My commands! Then blessings would have flowed for you like a stream that never goes dry.

His commands are about a life the way God had it in mind when He created us!

In Isaiah 58:13–14, God gives us three clues on how to honor His Holy Day. I want you to think about all three of them. Now don't get discouraged and say, "I can never live up to that." Or, "I don't really see how that can possibly be practical in my life." Remember, these guidelines are given to make our lives better! Let's see how to apply them in our daily lives.

Traveling

We can honor God's day by not traveling.

That is a statement that almost seems weird in our

modern-day society. If we can't travel, we can't go any-where, and what good will it do to stay in the house for 24 hours? Slumping on the couch and watching television is not going to make your live better, is it? I am not going to give a definition on traveling versus moving. I am not going to discuss whether going to the beach is traveling, whether driving your car to church is traveling, or whether flying to a 3-day conference in Dallas, Texas, is traveling. It says in Colossians 2:16,

So let no one make rules about what you eat or drink or about holy days or the New Moon Festival or the Sabbath.

This book is not about rules; it is about guidelines and choices. The King James Version says, "*not doing thine own ways.*" Doing our own way is translated as traveling. That makes sense, doesn't it? Traveling is doing our own thing, not being concerned about others.

I simply want you to go back to Chapter 3 and think. I hope you have made up your mind about no longer pursuing your own interests on the Sabbath. I hope you came up with some things you can do that line up with God's interests. If you already have a vision on how that will change the Holy Day, the proposal not to travel, not to do your own thing, will be an easy one. Just ask yourself this question the moment you want to leave your house to go somewhere: Do I pursue God's interest with this?

It doesn't matter if you are about to get in the car

and drive to the mall, to the beach, to the theater, to a friend, or to church. Just take a moment and think; what is the reason for traveling? Is it for God, somebody else, or myself?

If for some reason you have been out of town on business, vacation, or on a family visit and you are thinking about driving or flying back on Sunday, take a minute and think. Is there a possibility to go back on Saturday or Monday? You may find that you have traveled many times without thinking about possible alternatives.

We should no longer ask ourselves if it is allowed to do certain things on the Sabbath, like the Pharisees did. The true question we should ask ourselves from now on should be: What am I pursuing? My own interests or God's interests? In this case, take the time to find out if there is a way to honor God's day by rearranging your (!) travel schedule.

Working

We can honor God's day by not working.

I am not going to discuss the ethics of working. This book is about trying to change the way you probably always lived. Working is simply something you do to earn a living or to support a household. When God says, "Do not work," He means, do not work—not for money and not to pursue your own interests. The King James Version calls it *"nor finding thine own pleasure."* Again, we should ask ourselves the following question: what am I pursuing? My own interests or God's interests?

If you are about to get something done on the Holy Day, you can ask yourself if you do pursue God's interest with this. Just wait a minute and think. If you have a paid job that requires you to work on weekends, ask yourself if it is really the dream job you want; maybe it wouldn't hurt to apply for something else or maybe you could ask your boss to be off on the Holy Day. You may find that you work many times without questioning yourself about the job.

Talking idly

We can honor God's day by not talking idly.

I am not sure if this is a word that is still being used. Personally, I had to look it up in the dictionary. God does not want us to talk idly on His day. A dictionary will give us many synonyms, but it all comes down to this: Do not talk worthless, useless, vain, futile, point-less or ineffective. We might have a tendency to talk 'bull' with our friends in school, with our coworkers, with our buddies in the gym, or with whomever and wherever. I don't think there is anything wrong with joking around. I don't think it is a sin to talk about nothing, so to say. In light of the Sabbath, however, God makes a clear and simple statement: You can honor My Day by not talking idly.

Ask yourself this simple question when you are about to open your mouth on His Day. What I am about to say, will it build me and the other person up? Not talking idly might be the most difficult of the three, but it will be the most rewarding too. Other people will notice the difference in your attitude, they will truly appreciate your effort, and you will meet more smiles and make more people happy than you can ever think of.

Meditate on the following:

❖ *Do I want my life to be changed? If yes, in what areas?*

❖ *Not traveling, working, and talking idly—what would be the most difficult for me and why?*

❖ *Do I think before I talk?*

Journal your thoughts:

Pray aloud:

Dear Father in Heaven, Thank you for giving me seven days a week to enjoy my life. I want to give to You what belongs to You. Thank you for giving me work, hobbies, and interests, for giving me things to do. Please help me to pursue Your interests, not out of obligation, but out of love. Holy Spirit, Help me to value and understand the Word every time I read it or hear it. Please help me to change my mind about always being busy.

Dear God, I want to dedicate my life to you with Your special day as the highlight of every week. Thank you for honoring me. You gave your first and only Son to save my life! What an awesome offer. I want to honor You. Thank you for guiding me into a better life with more time, more joy, and more fulfillment. I ask you, Holy Spirit, to help me rearrange my schedule according to God's plan. In Jesus' name, I ask this. Amen.

PART II

Then you will find the joy that comes from serving Me. I will make you honored all over the world and you will enjoy the land I gave to your ancestor, Jacob. I, the Lord, have spoken.

Isaiah 58:14

6

Then you will find the joy

Your commandments are my eternal possession; they are the joy of my heart.

Psalm 119:111

ॐ✝ॐ

Now we are getting to the easy part of this book, the blessing! After all that is God's part of the deal.

I want you to see and experience God's commandments as loving guidelines from a parent to a dear child. Maybe some of you were never able to look at His commandments that way because your parents or pastor or youth leader used to scare you with them. Maybe some of you are blind to the heart of God's commandments because all you can see is the punishment that may come when you won't obey. I urge you to read Psalm 119 from a translation that speaks to you. The writer is truly excited about God's Law, but that didn't come to him without effort. He prays for understanding in verse 33!

Teach me, Lord, the meaning of Your laws

I believe a lot of people find it hard to look at commandments that way because they don't look at it with the help of the Holy Spirit.

In Chapter 2, I compared our attitudes toward God's Word with the attitudes we use when handling an assembly manual. We get irritated before we even start reading. There are thoughts, preconceived thoughts, in our minds that tell us that what we are about to read will be hard and difficult to understand. In other words, our inner being fights before even attacked. This is simply another thing that God did foresee. That is why He gave us His Holy Spirit, who is also called the Helper. In 2 Corinthians 3:6 (NIV), we can see how the Spirit is able to bring life to the Scriptures.

He has made us competent as ministers of a new covenant—not of the letter but of the Spirit; for the letter kills, but the Spirit gives life.

Most of you probably remember rebelling at your parents' rules, thinking they were way old fashioned and not applicable in the century you lived in. You also know that most of their rules were there to protect you and give you a fair chance in life. Deep in your heart, you know most of their rules were even there because they loved you, and they did not want any harm to come to you.

Do you see and understand why our lives could be easier and more relaxed when we follow God's commandments? Reading the commandments with the Holy Spirit inside you changes everything. They rather sound like sincere advice then law enforcement regulations, advice that will bring success and blessings when applied. When we allow ourselves to read God's Word with an open mind, without going on the offensive before He even has finished His first line, and without preconceived ideas, we will discover that God is sincere in guiding us. He does not want us to get lost somewhere down the road of our lives. I cannot put enough emphasis on the fact that this book is not about salvation, forgiveness, getting to heaven, or receiving eternal life. This is not about being a better person than the one next to you. Nobody can ever earn his or her way into heaven by pleasing God. We will always fall short! Only God's grace and our faith can accomplish that. This book is about a better life while here on earth, a life in all its fullness. Remember John 10:10b? A life God had in mind when He created us in His image. This book is about how God, in the Old Testament, describes the way He wants us to live and about how Jesus, in the New Testament, explains to us how to do that.

In Matthew 12:7, Jesus discusses the Sabbath with a group of religious folks. He takes them back to the Old Testament where it says,

It is kindness that I want, not animal sacrifices.

This book is not about sacrifices, about do's and don'ts that will make our life complicated and maybe even miserable. This book is about love and kindness. Love, first of all toward the God who made us, and second, to the people around us. Jesus is the ultimate example on how to love the way God wants it. In Matthew 5:17 (NIV) He says,

Do not think that I have come to abolish the Law or the Prophets; I have not come to abolish them but to fulfill them.

We can discuss and debate the Ten Commandments, and in this case, the keeping of the Sabbath, as long as we want, but when we look at the Law the way Jesus did, it suddenly makes sense. He came to fulfill it. We can do that too!

Being a Christian simply means being Christlike. Jesus is the example of a Christian life. Simply imitating Jesus without accepting His grace would lead us nowhere. Trying to obey His teachings without accepting the forgiveness of our sins would only lead to frustration. The Bible speaks very clearly about the position we all have in Christ, for example in Acts 15:11.

We believe and are saved by the grace of the Lord Jesus.

We need His grace! With our sinful nature, we could never, ever even come close to fulfilling the Law the way Jesus did. That is why Jesus shared our sin in order that we could share in His righteousness. There is an absolutely powerful Scripture about that concept in 2 Corinthians 5:21.

Christ was without sin, but for our sake God made Him share our sin in order that in union with Him we might share the righteousness of God.

Hallelujah! Once we have accepted God's grace, it turns out to be an honor to fulfill the Law in love, the way Jesus did. We will start pleasing God because we are thankful not because we are trying to be in a better position with Him. We will show our love to God, not by reading the letter, but by simply obeying it in life and love! Instead of going around telling people what they can and cannot do, we can do acts of love and kindness as described in Chapter 5 and fulfill what God had in mind. He promises in Deuteronomy 7:9 to:

Show His constant love to a thousand generations of those who love Him and obey His commandments.

He is serious about this deal!

Much of Scripture can be divided in two parts, basically the same way as this book, an Obedience part and a Blessing part. It is amazing how many Scriptures we can find where God gives us advice and promises something in return when we follow that advice. So let us get to God's part, the blessing! You want to be blessed, don't you?

Isaiah 58:14 starts with *"then you will find the joy . . ."* God promises us JOY! He promises a special kind of joy, as we will discover in the next chapter. For now, I want you to stop a moment and think about joy. The Bible talks about different kinds of joy that Christians can experience. Here are some of them:

a. The JOY of salvation
In Psalm 51:12, we can read about our greatest joy, the joy of salvation. Whether you have a sense of humor or not, whether you are an introvert or extrovert, whether you are rather pessimistic or not, you can experience the joy of salvation by simply asking for it as the psalmist did. Maybe you have asked, and see no joy in your life, The Bible says the joy of our

salvation can be restored. It is a gift from God Himself to us; it is a fruit of the Holy Spirit who dwells in us after we are born again, and it just needs to be cultivated and watered to make it grow!

b. The JOY of the Lord
In Nehemiah 8:10 (NIV) the prophet declares,

The joy of the Lord is your strength.

What a powerful statement! Nehemia says this to the people, because they had been weeping while listening to the Law being read. Do not be sad, be joyful, it is your strength! The Bible talks here about a joy that is not human; it is a divine kind of happiness and it will strengthen you!

c. The JOY of my heart
Are you ready for this one? Psalm 119:111 speaks about the joy of your heart. The psalmist speaks about his love for God's Law.

Your commandments are my eternal possession; they are the joy of my heart.

God's guidance should bring us joy. Not just a smile on our faces, but true joy in our hearts.

d. Everlasting JOY
Isaiah 51:11 (NIV) talks about everlasting joy that will crown the heads of the people who will return to Zion. He talks about a joy that will never stop. A joy that will last forever!

e. The JOY of serving Me

In the next chapter, you can read all about this joy. Of course, there is a lot more said about joy in the Bible. The book of Philippians, for example, is nicknamed the book of joy, because it speaks so much about the subject. Listen to Paul's words in Philippians 4:4 for example,

May you always be joyful in your union with the Lord. I say it again: rejoice!

What a wonderful Scripture.

Personally, I love the word joy. It means so much more than happiness. You can be happy because someone has been nice to you, because the sun is shining, or because you have received a present. Happiness is the result of certain circumstances or certain things done to or for you. How often do we say: Yes, that will make me happy. Something needs to be done to produce that feeling. Joy is something you have, regardless of the circumstance. You are happy, but you have joy. Happiness is the result of something happening to you; joy is the result of something that has happened in you. Joy is a possession; it doesn't come and go like happiness or even pleasure or enjoyment.

Let's say joy is divine happiness. Joy is part of God's divine character. He likes to share it with us through His Holy Spirit. In Galatians 5:22, we can learn what God's character is all about.

But the Spirit produces love, joy, peace, patience, kindness, goodness, faithfulness, humility and self-control.

Joy is a product of God's character in us. We HAVE

it, even if we don't feel happy. Happiness goes up and down with our circumstances; joy is permanent. It is a divine gift from God to us. Joy is a product of the Holy Spirit and does not depend on what other people do for us. It is something on the inside that is always present. That is why joy is so much better than just happiness; it lasts. Do you know anybody who always seems at peace and joyful, even if things go wrong? Do you wish you could have more joy and be less anxious?

The Bible promises us joy if we treat the Sabbath as sacred. It is no question whether we will have it or not. Isaiah 58:14 says: "*then you will find the joy.*" You will find it if you look for it. You will find it if you try. Finding something only occurs when we have been looking for it. You may be a Christian who claims to have the Holy Spirit inside, but yet you are not joyful. Is it possible that the Holy Spirit forgot to produce joy in your life? No! Joy will be there when the Spirit is present. That is a promise according to Galatians 5:22. Joy is a fruit that the Spirit produces in our lives. Sometimes we simply have to look for it.

I'll give you a practical example. You might have a garage or storage room with mountains of stuff in it that you don't even remember storing there. You do not know what you actually possess, just because you never go through the pile. You forgot! Sometimes that happens with the gifts God gave us. We pray, we ask, we whine, we receive, and we put it in storage. Isn't it time to organize our stuff? We may find long forgotten treasures. Joy is something to be treasured.

The specific joy that the Lord promises us here will be found only if . . . And for the "if," we have to go back to Isaiah 58:13 again and read the first five chapters of this book. Obedience and blessing—the two are tied together the way seed and harvest are tied together. You cannot have one without the other. Aren't you excited about teaming up with God? If we do our part, He will do His part.

Meditate on the following:

❖ *How do I see the Ten Commandments?*

❖ *Do I accept guidance and correction in my life? If yes, from whom?*

❖ *What gives me happiness? What takes away my happiness?*

Journal your thoughts:

7

That comes from serving Me

Remember that the Lord will give you as a reward what He has kept for his people. For Christ is the real Master you serve.

Colossians 3:24

ॐ†ॐ

In Isaiah 58:14, God promises that we will find the joy that comes from serving Him if we treat the Sabbath as sacred.

Serving God is a term commonly used in Christian circles, but less so in our daily world. Serving has become a term reserved for the work certain people do in restaurants. Servers or waitresses, for that matter, are occupations. They do it because they get paid for it. Do we know what it means to serve the Lord? When talking about someone who serves the Lord, do we think about a pastor in a big, big church, a volunteer who works with the poor and homeless, an evangelist who works in third-world countries, or a teenager who gave up a year of his life to go abroad to Bible school? What does it mean to serve the Lord, and if we do serve Him, is it possible to find joy in that?

HOW do we serve the Lord in our daily life? How do we put that into practice? I will give plain, simple, and biblical ways to serve God in your church and in your daily life. You can start putting them into practice today.

First of all, we need to keep in mind that we are not asked to serve God because He needs anything from us. In Acts 17:25, we can find a powerful statement.

Nor does He need anything that we can supply by working for Him, since it is He Himself who gives life and breath and everything else to everyone.

God does NOT need our service, but He wants us to serve others. That is what He loves! We can find ways to serve the Lord throughout the whole Bible. In Deuteronomy 10:12–22, we are given an account of serving God in different ways. Verse 12b says,

Love Him, serve Him with all your heart, and obey all His laws.

Loving, serving and obeying cannot be separated. I want to put it this way: Out of LOVE for God, we will SERVE others, and in doing so, we'll OBEY Him.

In Deuteronomy 10:12–22, we will find that God mixes service to Him with service to other people. We simply cannot love God and not love our neighbor. We cannot love our neighbor without loving God. We can try, but we will find it very hard. Serving God has always two sides to it: Him and others. We can read this in Matthew 22:37–40, where Jesus answers one of the Pharisees who came to Him with a question.

Love the Lord your God with all your heart, with all your soul, and with all your mind. This is the greatest and the most important commandment. The second most important commandment is like it: Love your neighbor as you love yourself. The whole Law of Moses and the teachings of the prophets depend on these two commandments.

When reading Jesus' words, it becomes clear why we cannot obey God without love. To love is to obey! Just reading the commandments and keeping them to the letter is not what Jesus asks. He wants us to fulfill them in love.

In Deuteronomy 10, verse 19, God says,

So then, show love for those foreigners, because you were once foreigners in Egypt.

God speaks about showing love to foreigners. He is trying to teach us a principle that Jesus repeats in Matthew 7:12.

Do for others what you want them to do for you: this is the meaning of the Law of Moses and of the teachings of the prophets.

Do you have a new person in your class? Treat him nice and make him feel welcome, for you were once a newcomer yourself. Is there a new colleague at work? Help him to find his way, introduce yourself, and make him feel comfortable at the new workplace, for you stepped into that office a first time too. Have new immigrants moved into your neighborhood? Welcome them, shake their hand, bake a pie, and take it over, for you were once a stranger in town.

Maybe you notice a first time visitor in your church. Walk up to that person and welcome him or her. My husband and I visited different churches in America, before we started to attend the Solid Rock Christian Center in Ventura, CA. We noticed that the friendly treatment of first time visitors is much better in traditional churches then in evangelical, nondenominational churches. It could be that the traditional ones are more anxious to get new members, but still, shouldn't we all work hard to make strangers feel at home?

Do you see how easily we can translate these principles of serving into our daily routine and life? In the same chapter, Deuteronomy 10, God speaks about reverence and faithfulness to Him in verse 20.

Have reverence for the Lord your God and worship only Him. Be faithful to Him and make your promises in His name alone.

God reminds us to be as serious about Him as He is about us. Ask yourself if you worship others than Him. Maybe it is your partner, your movie idol, your favorite baseball player, maybe your job, or your money that is getting more attention and time than God. Ask yourself if you are faithful to God. Did you promise Him to attend church regularly, to pray every day, or to study a particular part of Scripture every day? Are you faithful to your promises? If you find it hard to keep all your promises to God, start with one promise, and keep it until it becomes part of your daily life, like getting dressed, eating, and drinking.

Romans 12 is a chapter in the Bible describing life in God's service. It offers a lot of possibilities to serve God in spiritual as well as practical ways. Verse 11 and 12 for example:

- *Work hard and do not be lazy.*
- *Serve the Lord with a heart full of devotion.*
- *Let your hope keep you joyful,*
- *be patient in your troubles, and*
- *pray at all times.*
- *Share your belongings with your needy fellow Christians, and*
- *open your homes to strangers.*

Again, can you see how God mixes service to Himself and to others? Praying without helping others is not what He has in mind nor helping others without praying. You may pray, Lord, help my friend with his homework. I know he is struggling. You may pray and pray. Don't you think God wants YOU to help that person? So many of our prayers are questions. Lord, will you do this and that? Many times the solution, the answer, is in our own hands. We just have to do what we have to do—serve others! Go and help that friend and pray for guidance.

Do you know somebody in church who needs a pickup truck to move some items? Maybe you can lend yours to him or do the job with him. Do you know of somebody who does not have access to the Internet and wants to send some e-mails? Offer your help and computer skills for an afternoon. Are some folks from out of town visiting your church? Maybe they can stay at your place. Just try to put into practice what the Bible says. Reading and living God's Word are totally different things. Work and pray, pray and work!

Being joyful and being patient are ways of serving the Lord too! If others can see, we are joyful under circumstances that normally require super strength and courage. If others can see, we are patient under circumstances that normally require self-discipline and special kindness. They will recognize Christ in us and that brings glory to God.

We can also serve God by serving His church. He loves it when we get involved the way He has in mind. 1 Corinthians 12:5 explains this.

There are different ways of serving, but the same Lord is served.

The Bible shows us in 1 Corinthians 12 how we can serve God in our church. Verse 6 says,

There are different abilities to perform service, but the same God gives ability to everyone for their particular service.

1 Corinthians 12:8–10 provides a list of nine gifts as given by the Holy Spirit to Christians. They are needed for building up the church! God's church

(whether local or universal) is a living organism. It moves, it grows, and it changes. The Bible uses the metaphor of a human body with all its different parts. As humans, we don't merely exist; we LIVE! We take care of our body, we feed it well, we exercise it if we want to keep it in shape, we grow, and we change, etc. The church needs the same kind of attention in order to grow and become beautiful and gracious.

I realize this chapter gives only a short list of all the ways that we can use to serve the Lord. I would like to urge you to find ways to serve the Lord by reading the Bible. If you have a Bible with a concordance (that is a word list) just look up the word service or serving and start reading the Scriptures. You will find simple ways of doing little acts of love and kindness during the day. As explained in this book, serving the Lord basically has three aspects to it:

1. Serving God
2. Serving others
3. Serving His church

God promises us joy when we serve Him. By now, you will see that joy will not come when we do things out of duty, fear, or peer pressure. Joy from serving comes when we do it out of love! God has set it up that way; if we obey Him because we love Him, He will reward us. We will just want to do more and more for Him! Serving will become a desire of our hearts! Treating the Sabbath as sacred will become a desire of our heart, too, and it will bring joy, unspeakable joy. It doesn't take long to find out how easily that works. We do something for God out of love. He rewards us with joy, and because we find so much joy in doing that for Him, we want to do more for Him. In other words, we will discover that we just love serving Him!

Meditate on the following:

❖ *What does it mean to me when someone serves the Lord?*

❖ *Who or what do I serve on a daily basis and how?*

❖ *What promise do I want to make to God and what do I need to do to keep that promise?*

Journal your thoughts:

8

I will make you honored all over the world

And My Father will honor anyone who serves Me

John 12:26b

ও✝ও

The promised blessing in Isaiah 58:14 has a double function. It contains personal blessings as well as a corporate blessing.

In the previous chapters, the first personal blessing has been discussed, namely the joy that comes from serving God. In the next chapter, the second personal blessing will be discussed. Namely, we will enjoy the land God gave to our ancestor, Jacob. Both blessings deal with joy. God promises joy to those who treat His Sabbath as sacred. God also promises honor. "I will make you honored all over the world" sounds more like a blessing for a whole nation or a group of people than for an individual. It has a prophetic ring to it. I would like to call that the corporate blessing.

As a European, currently residing in the USA, I meet a lot of Americans who think or feel and express the feeling that they are not honored in the rest of the world. They are afraid that people think negatively about them because of economic and political views. Many times people ask me, "What do you Europeans think about us? Do people like us over there?" Maybe you have never asked that question to a foreigner, but I noticed that in general, people do really care what others think and say about them as a nation. That is why it is so interesting to read what God promises the people who honor His Holy Day: I will make you honored all over the world. That is an awesome promise, isn't it? I want you to think of this as a promise that God not only made to the Israelites but to all future believers. It is a promise He makes today to those who treat the Sabbath as sacred.

I remember when America was honored all over the world. As a child, I heard the heroic stories about World War II, about our liberators, and about people offering their lives for our freedom. America hasn't changed her liberation policy, but somehow she is no longer honored all over the world. Is it possible that the worldwide honor has disappeared because we no longer honor God's Holy Day? After promising us joy, He almost casually adds His next promise in Isaiah 58:14, the corporate blessing:

I will make you honored all over the world.

This chapter has probably been the hardest one to write. I had so many questions. I asked God, for example, who He has in mind when He says "I will make you honored all over the world." I also asked Him how He was going to do that. If I read that Scripture as an individual, it is hard to imagine how God is going to honor me all over the world. Who knows my name? How do I get across to other continents? If I read it for the country I live in, I wonder if He wants to make that whole nation honored all over the world or maybe just all the Christians or certain churches? How is honoring going to take place on a worldwide scale? I understood that the "how" is not up to us; that is up to Him. The "who" will be solved when the honoring starts to happen.

The first Scripture that came to my mind was Luke 6:38b,

The measure you use for others is the one that God will use for you.

We will be honored the way we honor God and others. In Chapter 4, I talked about giving value to God's Holy Day and honoring it. Value and honor are personal. According to Luke 6:38b we decide which measure God is going to use for us. As I wrote at the beginning of this chapter, there is a prophetic ring to this part of Scripture. Do you dare to think about the promised consequences of honoring God's day on a small scale, a bigger scale, or even a world scale?

I have tried.

Local church scale

I would like to use an example that I have seen recently. Rick Warren's popular book *A Purpose Driven Life* is currently used on an international scale to promote spiritual growth in churches through Bible study groups. His Saddleback Church in Lake Forest, California, became a practical example for spiritual development and is for that reason honored all over the world, at least by the readers of this book.

Now back to honoring the Sabbath. Let's say, as a

church, you decide that from now on you will try to value the Holy Day and honor it in the way described by Isaiah. What will be the result? Well, apart from the extra time that each person will gain and the joy that you will experience, the whole church will receive God's corporate blessing. They will be honored all over the world. Like Rick's church, you might set an example for many, many other churches to follow. People might come for advice and encouragement. You might be invited to other churches to talk and help them to honor the Sabbath in a way that is a joy for everybody. You might exchange ideas and experiences. Like I said before, I don't know exactly how God is going to do it, but I know He sure is capable of keeping His promise!

Christian scale

Do you dare to think big? What if Christians (in the USA) decided to start valuing and honoring the Sabbath again? Millions and millions of people will gain extra time, will find joy, and will be honored all over the world. Before I visited the USA for the first time, the only picture I had was what I had seen on television and in movie productions. To be honest with you, it was not a pretty picture! Hollywood didn't exactly do her best to make America honored all over the world. A portrait of sex, crime, drugs, and violence has been widely spread. Most of the time that is the only picture people have of this country. I grew up in Holland, and I know that the only picture many foreigners have is the one of windmills, wooden shoes, prostitution, and marijuana. I talked to people who actually thought that we drink tulip juice in Holland. Images are created by the media, and they are not always doing a good job. They only show us what they want us to see. In other words, we see a colored picture.

When God says that He can make us honored all over the world, we can be sure that He will do a better job then the media or use the media to do a better job. Maybe the time has come to bring about another picture of this part of American life. Christian America can indeed set an international example on how to honor God; it will be contagious! The time has come to get rid of bad examples. We need to replace the stories of fallen television preachers and lustful priests with stories of people who have real joy in serving God, because they decided to start honoring His commands. This Christian movement will start in the USA and spread all over the world—a Bible-based refreshment in Christianity with the USA as birthplace! Think about it. Don't you think God is able to honor us all over the world?

Nationwide scale

Wow, this kind of thinking asks for courage and maybe the ability to dream big! What if nonbelievers could see the change in the lives of those Christians who lovingly honor the Sabbath? What if they could see the peace, the joy, and the fulfillment? What if the government decided to change some rules? Let me explain. In Holland, Christians do not make up the majority of the population, but Sunday is, by most people, regarded as a day of rest. Stores, businesses, and shopping malls are closed. As a matter of fact, they all close on Saturday at around 6 o'clock, and do not open up until midday Monday, so everybody can enjoy a real day's rest. There is less traffic on the freeways and a lot of families spend time together. Of course, these practices were founded by our religious forefathers and are still intact because our royal family values the Bible and our governments somehow never completely succeeded in wiping out our Calvinistic background. It hurts me to see that slowly, slowly society is changing and turning into a 24/7 chaos as well. Some cities decided to have shopping Sundays once a month. Some stores stay open until Saturday evening at 8 o'clock. I know this does not sound alarming to people who are used to a 24/7 society, but in Holland, it resulted in strong arguments and political debates.

Is it possible, as a nation, to turn from promoting a 24/7 society as the ultimate, free lifestyle to a society that finds her freedom in taking a day of rest after every six days? Is it possible to find more time by doing less? Is it possible to turn from a busy, busy lifestyle that many of us have adapted as normal, to a peaceful and joyful one? Is there truly a way out of our hectic schedule? Well, it doesn't hurt to admit that we made a mistake; it is not too late to turn back. America could be a nation that would set an example for all other nations.

God wants to make us honored all over the world!

Meditate on the following:

❖ *If applicable, how do I feel when visiting other countries?*

❖ *Do I have a role model in my life? If yes, who is she/he and what do I appreciate in her or him?*

❖ *What is the biggest thing that I have seen God doing?*

Journal your thoughts:

9

You will enjoy the land I gave to your ancestor, Jacob

*You should realize, then, that the real descendants of
Abraham are the people who have faith.*

Galatians 3:7

৵✝ৎ

This is the part of Scripture that really stood out
for me, when I read it that morning at the breakfast
table. It answered a lot of my questions.

As with most other verses applied in this book, I
looked up the NIV and KJV translations too. The
NIV translated it this way:

*. . . and I will cause you to ride on the heights of the land
and to feast on the inheritance of your father Jacob.*

I would like to give you the interpretation of this
verse as I read it in the TEV, the way the Holy Spirit
showed it to me and translated it into my present-
day thinking.

When reading the Bible, I rely upon the guidance
of the Holy Spirit, the same Spirit who inspired the
authors at that time, in order to understand what
God wants to teach me. I simply ask God to open
my eyes for His Word the way the Psalmist did in
Psalm 119:18,

Open my eyes, so that I may see the wonderful truths in Your Law.

I know it is necessary for my spiritual eyes to be opened for the secrets of God's Word. Jesus did the same thing for the disciples as we can read in Luke 24:45. What a wonderful and powerful event;

Then He opened their minds to understand the Scriptures.

It is a turning point in the Bible. Jesus then tells His disciples to wait for the power of the Holy Spirit to come down upon them. We know that after Jesus' departure it is indeed the power of the Spirit that opens our eyes. 1 Corinthians 2:10 explains a bit more about the function of the Holy Spirit.

The Spirit searches everything, even the hidden depths of God's purposes.

A little bit further, in verse 12, the Bible explains why we have received the Spirit.

We have not received this world's spirit; instead, we have received the Spirit sent by God, so that we may know all that God has given us.

So that we may know all that God has given us! The Bible is God's gift to us, and He wants us to meditate on it, to get familiar with it. It is the Holy Spirit who makes the Bible so interesting. He gives life to the Bible. No matter if we read it literally, practically, historically, spiritually, or symbolically, it is the Holy

Spirit who will teach us the true meaning. Jesus talks very plainly, yet so powerfully, about the work of the Spirit in John 14:26.

The Helper, the Holy Spirit, whom the Father will send in My name, will teach you everything and make you remember all that I have told you.

What an awesome promise!

The Bible is a dimensional book. There is always a deeper side to it than we can see. The message is always powerful and the Spirit will teach us everything. That is why I would like to give you the interpretation I received, as well as a simple (I am by no means a scholar) symbolical interpretation of the same verse as I read it in the NIV and KJV. However you look at them, they both hold a promise, a blessing!

Since 1989, my husband and I have been visiting the USA on and off. We did a lot of traveling all over the world, with the mainland USA and California (as well as some neighboring states) as one of our favorite hangouts. It did not take long to figure out that the way we lived was not the so-called American way. We both worked seven or eight months a year in Holland, saved up some money, and traveled the rest of the year all over the world. As a result of that, we never had permanent jobs, didn't do career building, and certainly have no pension to look forward to.

We noticed that the common way of thinking in the USA is to work as hard and as much as we can, retire early, and then start enjoying life. (I write this with the following notion: Exceptions to the rule are always there.) We always thought this was kind of odd. Why postpone enjoyment of life until the day it might be hard to enjoy because of age or health issues. That did not make sense.

For years and years, we absolutely enjoyed the beauty of America's many parks and nature reserves. We often said: God truly saw that it was good when He made America! This country has been blessed with incredible nature, for us it is one of the most beautiful and diverse countries in the world.

Whenever we would rave about that beauty to someone in the store, at the gas station, or wherever, the response would almost always be, "Well, you guys have seen more of this country than me." A lot of people we met had never been out of state! Now we know that not everybody has the desire to travel. Some folks are just downright happy to be at home. Nevertheless, a commonly used excuse is, I don't have time to travel now. I am always working to pay my bills. Maybe one day when I retire . . . I am too busy now.

Thoughts about the American way of living were the first ones that came to my mind when I read the part in Isaiah 58:14 where God promises the people who treat his Sabbath as sacred the ability to enjoy the land. I know this Scripture talks about the land that God gave to our ancestor Jacob, and I know that wasn't the USA, but let's take a look at Galatians 3:7.

You should realize, then, that the real descendants of Abraham are the people who have faith.

When the Bible talks about the real descendants of Abraham, and thus Jacob, the Bible is talking about the believers! Abraham, Isaac, and Jacob are our ancestors too! Whether you agree with this interpretation or not, I will try to give you the vision I have. The reason why many do not enjoy the land that was given to us is the fact that we don't take a day of rest every seventh day and dedicate it to the Lord! Now I didn't make that up; it is what this Scripture says. I just made it personal for the country that I am living in at this moment.

Why would God make such an incredible, beautiful country for millions of people? To merely exist and work as slaves? To build houses just about everywhere? To pollute nature? Do you think He had a retirement community in mind when He shaped the Sierra's, when He formed the beaches and when He created the forests? Do you think our excuses to postpone enjoyment of what He made for us, by about 50 years, will impress Him? Even if you are not an outdoors person, there are tons of possibilities to enjoy the land that was given to you—reading a book at the beach, having a family BBQ in the park, visiting a rose garden, anything!

Now you might not feel comfortable with this way to interpret the Scriptures. You may feel this is not what God had in mind when He spoke to the Israelites. You may even think this Scripture has nothing to do with the way we live today. Well, the Bible certainly has to do with the lives we are living today. Think about it for a moment. We can make the Bible as personal as we want. As I wrote in the beginning of this book, don't read this with the word "history" all over it; apply it to your daily life. The Bible is God's living Word, it can and will speak to you today. If you read this Scripture, what thoughts come to your mind? How do you read it?

Be honest. Do you enjoy the land, state, county, town, or house you live in? Do you appreciate its beauty, the space, the variety? Would you like to spend more time doing fun things, but are you always busy? Have you been thinking about horseback riding, play-ing golf, kayaking or starting a flower garden, but it seems you cannot find the time? Do you see where I am going with this? It all comes down to what I wrote in Chapter 3. If we start honoring and valuing God's Holy Day, we will always have enough time to get everything done. Not just enough time to get everything done, but we will also enjoy where we live and how we live! God clearly promises us the joy that comes from serving Him and enjoyment of the land we live in. Now isn't that a comforting promise?

So maybe you find the preceding interpretation of this Scripture far fetched; maybe it is not the way Scripture is commonly explained. Personally, I believe that a lot of people are not being able to enjoy where they live because they do not honor the Sabbath. I know this is a bold statement, and I am glad the thought didn't come from nowhere. It is how I read that particular Scripture in Isaiah 58, and it is how the Holy Spirit explained it to me. I realize of course that a lot of people are happy where they live and how they live. I understand it is not possible to apply a Scripture like this to everyone and suggest that we are all struggling with the same issues. As I stated at the beginning of chapter 2, God speaks to us personally, but He also speaks to a nation that reads His Word. He speaks to a generation that is struggling with stress and too little time to get everything done. I am sure you will know right in your spirit if this is about you or not!

I just want us all to think about our personal situations. Are we truly happy and satisfied with where we live and how we live, or is there deep, down inside that longing for more. If only I could buy that house, that boat, that car. If only I had more time. If only I had visited more countries. Very often we think that reaching our next goal will bring us closer to fulfillment of our dreams, but will there ever be an end to our feeling of lack? Is it possible to enjoy who we are, where we are, and what we are in life without having to add?

I believe that when we start to honor and value His Holy Day, we will find that the rest of the week will be blessed too. We will find joy in serving God, and we will truly be able to enjoy where we live. We will be able to see God's hand in it.

I promised to give you a symbolical interpretation of this Scripture too. When God says that you will enjoy the land that He gave to your ancestor, Jacob, he is talking about the blessing as promised to Abraham, Isaac, and Jacob.

In Genesis 12:2, you can read about God's first promise to Abram. (His name wasn't changed yet).

I will give you many descendants, and they will become a great nation. I will bless you and make your name famous, so that you will be a blessing.

As Abram moves on with his life, God keeps repeating His promise to him and later on to his son Isaac and his grandson Jacob. In Genesis 15:1 God speaks again.

Do not be afraid, Abram. I will shield you from danger and give you a great reward.

In Genesis 28:10–22, you can read about Jacob's famous stairway to heaven and encounter with God. In verse 15, God's says,

Remember, I will be with you and protect you wherever you go, and I will bring you back to this land. I will not leave you until I have done all that I have promised you.

One of the highlights in this story can be found in Genesis 35, where God blesses Jacob again. Verse 11 and 12 are holding the promises:

I am Almighty God. Have many children. Nations will be descended from you, and you will be the ancestor of kings. I will give you the land which I gave to Abraham and to Isaac, and I will also give it to your descendants after you.

Many, many years passed, and after the death of Jacob's son Joseph, the Israelites were treated very cruelly in Egypt where they were held in slavery. It was Moses who was called by God to rescue them out of slavery and bring them to the Promised Land.

A symbolical interpretation of the Scripture in Isaiah 58:14, as I see it, can be as follows: Egypt symbolizes the old, sinful life of humans before they become Christians. The Promised Land is the new life that you can have after being joined with Christ, also known as life in the Kingdom. Ephesians 2:6 states,

In our union with Christ Jesus He raised us up with Him to rule with Him in the heavenly world.

Now, when God says that you will be able to enjoy the land that was given to you He is talking about your spiritual life while being on earth—the life you received through your faith in Jesus Christ. The life you received when you left your old life behind, which you symbolically do when you are baptized in water. We can find this in Romans 6:4.

By our baptism, then, we were buried with Him and shared His death, in order that, just as Christ was raised from death by the glorious power of the Father, so also we might live a new life!

Isaiah 58:13–14 in other words tells us: when you obey God, He promises you an uplifting of your spiritual life. You will actually feel at home in the Kingdom!

You see, it doesn't matter how you read this Scripture. A promise is a promise. You can take it spiritually, symbolically, or both. Ask the Holy Spirit to help you.

I hope and pray that by now you have a clear idea how to please God. Ephesians 5:10 urges us,

Try to learn what pleases the Lord.

Remember, we should not be pleasing God to get things done from Him or to become better people. We should be pleasing God because we love Him, because we respect Him, and because we are thankful for His love for us! Remember when you where in love for the first time? You probably did the silliest things to please your love. You probably went out of your way just to be with that person. Maybe you listened to music together that you didn't even like; maybe you saw movies together that weren't your choice. You didn't even care. Nothing was too crazy to get her or his attention. Being in love with God means getting out of our way to please Him! We just love pleasing Him! Don't you think it is rather crooked to say that you love the Lord and at the same time refuse to do what pleases Him? That wouldn't work in human relationships. When you love somebody, you like to please that person, even if it was just to see a smile on their faces.

Treating the Sabbath as sacred is just one way of pleasing God. One way with many blessings attached. Of course, He gave us many ways to please Him. Think about the 10 Commandments as a whole, which of course are all summed up by Jesus in one new commandment. You can read in John 15:11–12,

I have told you this so that My joy may be in you and that your joy may be complete. My commandment is this: love one another, just as I love you.

That pleases God!

Meditate on the following:

❖ *Do I enjoy the place, whether it is my job, my home, my country, that God has given me?*

❖ *What natural and spiritual improvements do I want in my life?*

❖ *Do I love God? Do I want to please God?*

Journal your thoughts:

10

I, the Lord, have spoken

When He spoke, the world was created

Psalm 33:9

ॐ✝ॐ

Never before would I have thought it possible to write so much about just two verses in the Bible. It tells me something about the enormous impact of God's words.

If just two verses give enough inspiration for a book, just imagine how many books are hidden in the Bible! People get inspired every day, all over the world, when they read God's Word. Reading about God must be like being with Jesus. The gospel of John ends with these words

Now, there are many other things that Jesus did. If they were all written down one by one, I suppose that the whole world could not hold the books that would be written!

Wow, what a privilege to have walked and worked with Jesus! Every day must have been so exciting. If only we could have been alive when Jesus walked the earth. When He performed miracles and taught His disciples how to pray. It would be so much easier to believe in all those things. Well, maybe Jesus doesn't walk the earth in human form right now, but He certainly still works miracles and teaches people through the Holy Spirit and the Bible. If we apply the Word of God in our daily lives, it will be like walking with Jesus. It will be like having our teacher right there with us. 2 Timothy 3:16–17 says,

All Scripture is inspired by God and is useful for teaching the truth, rebuking error, correcting faults, and giving instructions for right living, so that the person who serves God may be fully qualified and equipped to do every kind of good deed.

Yes, as Christians we can be fully equipped to do our work if we use the Bible for guidance.

That is why throughout this book I asked you to read the Bible as if God is speaking to you today! In other words, personalize what you read. The Bible may be an old book, but it is the only book that is truly alive, simply because God inspired it! God's spirit is in it! That is why you can apply old principles, sayings, wisdom, or teachings from the Bible in your life today, and they will still work! The Bible is a handbook. We are supposed to do what it says, not just read it and forget about it. The Bible only works if we work it! God ends His deal in Isaiah 58:13–14 with the words,

I, the Lord, have spoken.

The NIV translation says it this way,

The mouth of the Lord has spoken.

The words that come from the mouth of the Lord are food for our spiritual lives. They will nourish our souls, like natural food nourishes our bodies.
In Deuteronomy 8:3 (NIV), the Israelites learned that when they were on their way to the Promised Land, just eating natural food wasn't enough.

He humbled you, causing you to hunger and then feeding you with manna, which neither you nor your fathers had known, to teach you that man does not live on bread alone but on every word that comes from the mouth of the Lord.

Yes, we need to feed our natural bodies in order to grow, stay healthy, and be strong. People with eating disorders know how true this is. Not eating, eating too much, or eating the wrong things will cause ailments, pains, and sickness. It will cause physical as well as mental imbalance. When not taken care of properly, the person could eventually die of these inflictions. In the same way, we need spiritual food to grow in our spiritual lives. We cannot claim to be a Christian without having Jesus Christ in our lives, because without Him we wouldn't be able to grow. Not growing means slowly dying. Jesus referred to Himself as the living bread in John 6:35.

I am the bread of life, Jesus told them. He who comes to Me will never be hungry, he who believes in Me will never be thirsty.

The word of God is not only nourishment for our souls, but it is also a weapon against the enemy, Satan, who tries to steal, kill, and destroy our lives.

Jesus used the same words from Deuteronomy 8:3 to get rid of the devil who wanted to trap and mislead Him. In Matthew 4:4 He answers the devil with the following words,

The Scripture says, 'Man cannot live on bread alone, but needs every word that God speaks.'

Note that Jesus says that we NEED every word that God speaks. God's word nourishes our soul, fights the devil, and builds up our faith.

I pray and hope that while reading this little book you have discovered the power of God's Word. God's Word is fulfilled in Jesus; that is such an awesome miracle. No other book in the Bible opens up as powerful as the gospel of John. No matter how many times I read it, it leaves me speechless. Just listen to verse 1–4.

Before the world was created, the Word already existed; He was with God, and He was the same as God. From the very beginning the Word was with God. Through Him God made all things; not one thing in all creation was made without Him. The Word was the source of life, and this life brought light to mankind.

John 1:14 reveals that the Word was Jesus.

The Word became a human being and, full of grace and truth, lived among us.

All God's words were personified in Jesus. Everything God said was fulfilled in His Son. Earlier in this book, we saw that God's laws are fulfilled in Him too. Jesus showed us the way to a better life. Jesus IS the way to a better life!

I have taken one of God's commandments out of its birthplace in history and put it in our daily lives at the dawn of the 21st century. I have put it smack in the middle of a time in which the Ten Commandments are the reason for public debates, lawsuits, and political turmoil. I am aware of a movement that is trying to get rid of the Ten Commandments in America's courthouses, judicial system, and schools. I am even more aware that we serve a God who wants the Ten Commandments back in America's homes, in America's family lives, and in the hearts of the people. It is from there that we will be able to change the world we live in. It is from within her own people that America can turn back to moral and high value living, the way God had in mind when He created us in His image!

I pray that keeping a Holy Sabbath will change the way we live and that it will give everyone a bigger desire to please God! I do not have to prove that God's Word still works today; it will prove itself.
I like to end this book with the same words that opened it in Chapter 1, the words of Jesus in Matthew 13:9,

Listen, then, if you have ears!

Meditate on the following:

❖ *In what areas of my spiritual life did I grow last year?*

❖ *How can I treat God's Word as food for my soul?*

❖ *By what morals do I live?*

Journal your thoughts:

Pray aloud:

Dear Father in Heaven, thank you for keeping Your part of the deal, for promising me joy. Thank you for being a God that wants to bless me because You love me. I want to bless You because I love You! Thank you for overseeing the world. You know me; You know every single person on earth. Holy Spirit, help me to keep my promises and help me to serve in many ways. I do not want to think of it as work, but as dedication and kindness! I ask you to change my attitude toward God's commandments. Please, open up my eyes for the Word so I can read it, love it, and LIVE it! I ask you to help me to dream big; I can make a difference in changing the world! Dear God, I want to do it Your way! Thank you for giving me a new life. Thank you for promising me enjoyment of all You've given me. Most of all, I want to love you the way You love me. Holy Spirit, help me to set my goals and to be obedient!
In Jesus' name, I ask this.
Amen.

For more copies of this book contact

TATE PUBLISHING, LLC

127 East Trade Centre Terrace
Mustang, Oklahoma 73064

(888) 361 - 9473

Tate Publishing, LLC

www.tatepublishing.com